FUEL
THE
SPARK

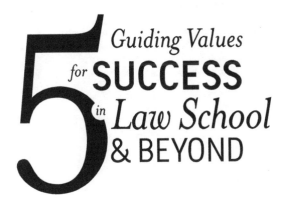

5 *Guiding Values* *for* **SUCCESS** *in* *Law School* **& BEYOND**

made**easy**
PUBLISHING

an imprint of Morgan James Publishing, LLC., New York

FUEL THE SPARK
5 Guiding Values for Success in Law School and Beyond

Library of Congress Cataloging-in-Publications Data
Library of Congress Control Number: 2008941914
Kevin E. Houchin, Esq
Fuel the Spark: 5 Guiding Values for Success in Law School and Beyond
ISBN: 978-1-60037-546-0
Library of Congress subject headings:
1. Law/Ethics 2. Professional Responsibility

Published by:

an imprint of Morgan James Publishing, LLC
1225 Franklin Ave. Ste 325
Garden City, NY 11530-1693
Toll Free 800-485-4943
www.MorganJamesPublishing.com

Design by Toolbox Creative: www.toolboxcreativecom.
Photography © 2008 TK Gujral: www.tekayegujral.com
Edited by Kari Palazzari.

DEDICATION

To Abra, Rune, Tobin, Merrick, Forrest, and
"The Man In The Yellow Coat."

Thanks to Kari Palazzari for her patience,
advice, and ruthless editing.

Special thanks, Tiffany, Dawn, Tom, Jim,
Braun, Matt, Ken, Joel, Jen, and Joe.

ENDORSEMENTS

Kevin Houchin has written a wonderful little guide book for law students. Too often, books about how to survive law school are replete with rules and suggestions about study, time management, and the like. Fuel the Spark is different. Kevin's book offers a different way of thinking about law school and your place in it as it offers thoughts about how you will develop as a person. Fuel the Spark is an insightful and enjoyable book, with stories and ideas which will stay with you throughout the three years of legal education.

> Joseph P. Tomain
> Dean Emeritus and Wilber & Helen Ziegler
> Professor of Law
> University of Cincinnati College of Law

The prescription that law students need!

> J. Kim Wright, Director,
> www.cuttingedgelaw.com

Such a quiet, yet profound missive. This book provides such a framework. I am encouraged that future legal practitioners will be able to avail themselves of this gentle aid to wake them up and live consciously at such a critical juncture in their personal and professional lives.

Idara E. Bassey, J.D., LL.M
www.OneLightMessenger.com
Author, Reflections of a Mystical Sistah

Kevin Houchin is the real deal. Kevin's stories are entertaining offering a message of hope and inspiration for lawyers and the legal profession. I wholeheartedly recommend Kevin to any organization considering hiring a speaker.

Tim Batdorf, Esq.
Attorney & Professional Coach
Past President, IAHL
www.lawyerandself.com

TABLE OF CONTENTS

PREFACE

> *"It is well known that lawyers suffer higher*
> *rates of depression, anxiety, and other mental*
> *illness, suicide, divorce, alcoholism and drug*
> *abuse, and poor physical health than the*
> *general population or other occupations...*
> *It is less well-known that these problems begin*
> *in law school."*

Best Practices for Legal Education, p. 30

Can you imagine your legal career as a fun, exciting, rewarding and balanced part of your larger life purpose? If you can, you're already on the right track to making the legal profession better than it is today. If you can't, then it's time to start and this book will help.

When I started thinking about law school, I bought every book I could find. Titles like *Slaying the Law School Dragon*, *Law School Confidential*, and *Planet Law School* became tactical resources for success in the law school classroom. Books like these tell you how to brief cases, introduce you to the Socratic method, and give you an overview of some of the required course material.

These books were helpful to me and they'll probably be helpful to you. But these books won't tell you how to balance all the challenges you'll face in law school while still holding onto the values and ideals you take to campus.

I was at a legal conference recently and we were asked to write down all the things we enjoyed about law school on sheets of yellow paper and all the things we hated about law school–things that hurt us emotionally–on pieces of pink paper. Out of 30 people, only I and one other person wrote anything on the "good" yellow sheets of paper. That's sad, but it's the norm.

Law school is notorious for taking bright, idealistic, values-inspired young (and not-so-young) people and turning them into something else. This doesn't happen to everyone, and it didn't happen to me. But it takes some conscious effort to avoid the common pitfalls of legal education. What separates those who end up with comments on the "good" yellow sheets? Context.

I'm definitely no smarter than any of my peers, and probably no smarter than you. But I was older when I started law school. I wasn't learning life out of a case book. I'd been married and divorced. I'd been through civil litigation. I'd worked for and been fired from companies. I'd started companies and failed. I'd started companies and succeeded. I'd bought and sold houses. I'd negotiated hundreds of contracts. I'd spent the previous three years traveling on business. When I quit my job to start law school I had plenty of time to do the work, but I also had time to think about the context within which I hoped to implement what I was about to learn.

That's the key to a successful and even fun law school experience: context. Even if you are not older or don't have as much life experience, my goal in this book is to give you that context through a short list of five simple, memorable values that will guide you to well-rounded, joyful success in your law school experience. If you keep the following 5 Guiding Values in your mind (or even better, taped to the top of your laptop, or as part of your computer screen background image) you'll be far more likely to keep the challenges of law school in balance with the rest of your life and your ideals. I guarantee it.

In fact, if you follow these guiding values and they don't help, just send this book back to me and I'll refund your money.

This book is short for several reasons. First, I want you to actually read it. If you're planning to go to law school, or are already in law school, you know how to read well, fast, and with high retention. You should be able to breeze through these chapters in short sittings. Second, you'll be reading a lot of material for class and I don't want to add to that burden. Third, I believe shorter books that get read again and again are more powerful than large tomes. Fourth, there are only 5 Guiding Values, which fits right into most people's short-term memory capabilities. I want these values to become second nature to you, and they won't if it takes too long to read the book.

We could argue about the words that describe the values—we're lawyers after all and questioning how other people classify thoughts is just part of our collective personality. We could add values to the list, and I'm sure you will. We could probably even reduce the list (NOT a typical lawyer trait). But I like having five principles because it's easy to remember the list by looking at the fingers on one hand. Finally, I believe everything you face in law school, and more importantly in your life after law school, fits nicely into one or more of these categories.

1. ACCEPT

The most profound choice in life is to either accept things as they exist or to accept the responsibility for changing them.

The Universal Traveler, page 41

You have just made a series of profound choices. There was something in your life that you didn't accept as it existed, so you accepted the personal responsibility to change that situation, and ended up in (or at least considering) law school. Similarly, something in your life led you to pick up this book.

It may seem silly to even think about this, but it's not. Many times we unconsciously and mistakenly "choose" to accept something the way it is when we really would rather have accepted the responsibility to change it. Those unconscious "acceptances" happen when we buy into assumptions.

Law school is full of underlying assumptions. Many of those underlying assumptions are promoted in the books I mentioned earlier. Your peers and professors will subtly reinforce many of these assumptions. Some are so subtle that you won't even realize you have accepted the premise until much later. For example, many law students think the only way they will be successful and happy after law school is if they land a six-figure job at a big-name firm right after graduation. To do that, you have to be in the top 10% of your graduating class (don't take my word for it, this requirement is right there on the interview sign-up sheets posted in the Career Services office) or at least be on the law review, moot-court board, or trial advocacy teams. To be sure, finishing in the top 10% of your class is a nice goal—and go for it if you can—but for the other 90% of you (us), defining success this way is going to lead to disappointment.

You don't have to accept the underlying premise that the only way to be happy after law school is to work in a big firm. I'm here to tell you that happy lawyers are often the exception rather than the rule in large-firm practice. Did you know that many large firms expect new associates to bill 2,000 hours per year? Do you know the costs of billing that many hours? It could cost you your health, your relationships, and your emotional stability. It's no wonder lawyers suffer from more mental health and substance abuse issues than the rest of society.

Of course, there are lots of lawyers who are happy at big firms and lots of young lawyers learn a great deal in those settings. My point is, the choice of career path is up to you. I never intended to work for a firm of any size. I planned to be a solo- or small-practice lawyer from the day I decided to accept my admission. That made it easier for me to reject the premise that the goal of law school is to land a job at a big firm, which, in turn, made it easier for me to set realistic goals about my grades.

You don't have to accept the premise that being in the top 10% of the class is the only way to be happy and helpful after law school. Don't get trapped into **unconsciously** accepting that notion. First and foremost, *you* decide what will make you happy after law school. Go ahead. Think about it. Write it down.

Do you feel better and in more control already? You *are* in control. Nobody else is going to accept the responsibility for your life.

That said, there are still lots of things you cannot control about law school–the first-year curriculum, grading on a curve, your professors, your classmates, the fact that one big final exam will determine your grade. No matter how much you complain, you will most likely have to just accept these aspects of your legal education. Nevertheless, you do have control over how you deal with these things. You can change your social and/or study groups, your level of involvement outside class, your second- and third-year schedules, and, most importantly, your outlook about life and law school.

The first step toward a balanced and healthy law school experience is to figure out what you want to get from it. Once you have a clear picture of your personal goals for law school, it becomes easier to sift through the things you must accept and the things you accept responsibility to change.

I was raised in a strict, traditional Christian family where questioning any form of authority was discouraged, so it took me a while to start questioning the important areas of my life. For the past several years, I've been intensively studying both the Western and Eastern spiritual practices, because we all base our unconscious assumptions on these religious and cultural traditions. As I spent time peeling back layers of this savory onion of thought, it became apparent that Western traditions tend to teach a philosophy of "make it happen," while the Eastern traditions tend to teach "let it happen."

Movies including *"What the Bleep Do We Know,"* *"The Secret,"* and even *"The Matrix,"* *"Star Wars,"* and many others explore the concept that ideas are all of life. It's what we do, or don't do, with those ideas that matters. The Western idea of the law of attraction asks us to visualize what we want and let the universe manifest that vision as we act in our lives. This is a "make it happen" idea. The Eastern traditions say to step out of our visualization, empty our mind, and receive or "let it happen."

While studying, journaling, and meditating (thinking & praying) on these topics, the words "surrender" and "receive" kept coming up. I have a hard time surrendering–I'm a "never give up" kind of guy. I grew up on a hog farm outside Gravity, Iowa. Yes, "Gravity." (I achieved escape velocity.) Like many small boys in Iowa, I enjoyed wrestling and started pee-wee wrestling practice in second grade. One of the things my coach said has stuck with me: "Never surrender, never give up, you don't even sleep on your back." I still have a hard time sleeping on my back, and I still have a difficult time with the concept of surrender. So I went to the dictionary, which is something you'll get used to in law school.

"Surrender" has a lot of meanings, not just "give up" or "capitulate." It also means some very empowering things like *give away, release,* and *let go.* The breakthrough for me was understanding that I can *surrender* my anxiety without *giving up* my goals. You can too, even in law school. You've already begun to clarify your goals, which can greatly reduce your anxiety when it comes time to pick classes or sign up for interviews. But there's more you can do to cope with the day-to-day pressures that wear on your ideals and your outlook. It's possible to surrender or "release" that negative pressure.

The best way to work with surrender is to tie surrender with its polar concept: "receive." We all like to receive. But sometimes we have a hard time receiving. I feel guilty when I receive. Letting someone else buy lunch or a round of drinks was uncomfortable to me. I had to move through that guilt and learn that surrendering and receiving are part of a cycle.

I work with a professional coach, Tiffany Lehman. In one coaching session, I was talking about how there wasn't really a lot of stuff coming back to me. I wasn't receiving a lot. I said, "I thought if you give a lot, you receive a lot." Tiffany said, "It's not necessarily that way." I always give, give, give. It's a very "masculine" orientation to have energy flowing out of me. So, Tiffany said, "You know what? You've got the conduit full of energy going out; you need to make some space for good stuff to come back."

Professional coaching is something I strongly suggest for everyone, even while in law school. Tiger Woods is the best in the world and he still uses a coach. Coaches are accountability partners that help you get better without nagging. If you are interested in working with a coach, I know of two that have JDs and specialize in working with lawyers/law students. Tim Batdorf (www.lawyerandself.com) is outside of Detroit, and Betsy Gutting (www.betsygutting.com) is in the Seattle area. Both offer coaching programs via phone for law students.

So I started saying, "Okay. What are the things I want to come back? What are the things I want to bring *into* my life?" And I made a list. That list is below on the "receive" side of the chart. I like to receive creativity. I like to receive respect. I like freedom. Wealth would be nice. Love. Wisdom. Harmony. Health. All those are on my list. Then I said, "Okay, what needs to empty out of this space so that something can come in. What is the duality of each of those things?"

Take a few minutes to make your own list. Seriously, start right now thinking of the things that you would like to receive and write them down. You've got big goals. That's why you are in law school. You've also identified some things you can and cannot change about the law school experience. Now focus on those things you CAN change. What do you want? What quality or experience do you want to receive in each of those areas? What do you need to surrender in order to receive what you want?

Here are some of the areas I recognized in my life:

Receive	Surrender
Respect	Judgment
Freedom	Attachment
Wealth	Greed
Wisdom	Pride
Harmony	Envy
Creativity	Convention

I'll explain the story behind a few of these couplets and explore how they may be relevant to your law school experience and legal career.

Respect & Judgment

To gain respect, I have to surrender judgment. By "surrender judgment" I do *not* mean stop using good judgment, but rather stop judging people or circumstances. I represent artists, musicians, entrepreneurs, and a lot of people who could be considered the "New Age spiritual fringe." I have a wonderful client who makes a living channeling an archangel. Not every client can sit down with a lawyer and say they channel an archangel and feel comfortable. Did you roll your eyes? I can honestly say that I didn't. I think I said something like "Cool!" Rolling your eyes is a judgment response. For me to be respected by this client, I couldn't be sitting in judgment of her.

I have another client who wrote a great book about how her journey in life is part of a group reincarnation tied up with a very well known rock band. It really is a GREAT book, but again, not many lawyers today can suspend judgment and respect this client's work.

The guy down the hall from my office handles bankruptcies, and I'm betting that before clients can build a respect for him, they have to know he's not judging them or their situation. I'll bet it's the same with good divorce lawyers. I haven't practiced in every area of law, but I'm positive that we practicing lawyers will regain a lot of the respect that has been lost in the profession if we suspend our judgment of other folks (leave that to the people with the title "Judge") and focus on earning our clients' respect.

When you surrender judgment, you automatically open up to the possibility that the other person is worthy of respect. In turn, that makes it easier for the other person to open up to the possibility that you are worthy of respect. This is how the couplet works: to receive respect, you have to surrender judgment.

Freedom & Attachment

I love freedom. It's part of the reason I'm self-employed. To receive the joy I find in the freedom of self-employment, I had to surrender attachment to a regular paycheck. Not everyone can do that, and I'm not preaching that you should, I just really enjoy freedom.

Sometimes we're not even conscious of our attachments and I'm no exception. When I finished my undergraduate degree and got a job, the first thing on the list of to-do's was to save up and buy a house. I did and started a series of unconscious attachments to the "security" of having a house, mortgage, lawnmower, garage, landscaping projects, etc. I didn't even think about it.

I finally woke up. I remember the moment vividly. My personal awakening on this subject happened on a beautiful Saturday afternoon in October.

My house had five, thirty-year-old cottonwood trees on a one-third-acre lot. These are huge, wonderful trees, with great shade, but they dropped way too many leaves. I hate raking leaves. I really hated spending five or six of the most beautiful Saturdays each fall raking leaves and the next day being sore from raking leaves. Compound that by the fact that I live in one of the most beautiful natural areas in the world and have a wonderful wife and three great kids. Compound it even more by the fact I'm a college football fan and live in a college town. The leaves were stealing my life.

My wife was sick of maintenance too, so we decided to sell the house, move outside of town and rent a house. Yes, we took a hit financially, but our quality of life—measured by "freedom"—went shooting off the scale. My Saturdays in the fall no longer involve raking leaves. I had to give up my unconscious attachment to owning a house and understand that this "surrender" was simply the thing to do before I could "receive" the freedom to live the life I want to live.

I'm not saying you shouldn't own a house. I'm just saying you should make *conscious* choices about the attachments you hold.

Law students are used to being highly successful in almost every area of their lives. We received top grades as kids and in our undergraduate programs. We were leaders on campus or in our careers prior to law school. Entering law school is a bit like going to the pros after playing minor league ball, because now you're working with and against the best of the best. Sometimes you'll be on top and those will be great days. Sometimes you'll be lower on the chart and that will take some adjustment. Accept, right now, that you will not always be at the top of the list, maybe for the first time in your life, and there's no shame in that.

I knew I wanted one of my areas of practice to be copyright law. I really enjoyed copyright class, and I focused extra energy on the course and on studying for the exam. That course was one where I set my goal to be in the top 5% of the class. I didn't make it. I was a bit upset, so I went to the professor after the exam and asked what I could have done better. She simply (and wisely) allowed me to read the top exam. I was humbled. Our exams were handwritten in blue-books and this student had written at least three times as much as I had during the exam, completing full analysis on even the sub-points that I just couldn't physically write in the three-hour exam period. That's when I realized that there really are mutants that live among us and there was a speed-writing mutant in my copyright class. I thanked my professor for the grade I had received and walked out of her office knowing that I had done very well by comparison, that I knew my stuff just as well, but had been out-paced in an area that mattered in the grading, but wouldn't matter in practice.

You will meet mutants too; recognizing them is more difficult. When you accept that you don't have to be the best every time, it will give you a great sense of freedom and balance. It will make it easier for you to get out of the law school building and enjoy your life. You'll have a chance to build wonderful friendships that last well beyond your days on campus. *Surrender* your attachment to be on top all the time and you will *receive* the freedom to be happy with yourself during your law school experience.

Wisdom & Pride

This is a classic couplet for students of law and students of life. It doesn't take a lot of prose to say that if you're so proud that you think you know everything, you'll never receive any wisdom. To receive wisdom you have to surrender your pride and admit that there are things you don't know. Simple.

There's a great little esoteric book published in 1908 called *The Kybalion*. Two of my favorite sayings in the book are, "Where fall the footsteps of the Master, the ears of those ready for his Teaching open wide." And, "When the ears of the student are ready to hear, then cometh the lips to fill them with wisdom." In other words, you have to be open (surrender) in order to learn (receive).

Law school has plenty of areas that need improvement, but one of the things every law school does well is offer students a chance to gain wisdom. Obviously, you can gain wisdom from your professors. Usually it's easy to give up your pride relative to unfamiliar subject matter or charismatic professors in order to let their wisdom into your life. It's more difficult to give up your pride and let the wisdom of your classmates into your life. Look around you. These are smart men and women. Some have more life experience than you, some have less. Each of them has some wisdom for you if you simply surrender your pride and receive the gifts they can offer—whether they know they are teaching you or not.

★ ★ ★

The pairs of concepts, items, and emotions that we can receive and surrender are endless. What are your couplets? One of my friends said that, for her, "love" didn't go with "guilt." It went with "shame." Each of the couplets should be meaningful to you.

Take a few minutes and write out some of your couplets, don't worry about perfection, just start making the list. Think about those things you accept the responsibility to change. What do you want? What do you need to let go of in order to get what you want? Have fun and by the time you're done, the page will look like some kind of weird matching test from grade school. (Wouldn't it be great if they gave matching tests in law school!)

The word "accept" embodies the spirit of both "receive" (getting something) and "surrender" (letting things be). There are lots of things about law school you must simply accept because you cannot change them. But there are also many things you can change because you control your outlook, your goals, and your choices. To maintain balance in law school, you must first identify what you are willing to accept and what you are willing to accept the responsibility for changing. Then, identify what you must surrender in order to receive the change you want.

Consciously Accept. (Or Not)

It's the first guiding value.

Receive and Surrender Every Day

*While sitting quietly, mentally say "receive"
as you breathe in, and "surrender" as you
breathe out. Then start adding your couplets, for
example "Receive Wisdom" as you breathe in,
and "Surrender Pride" as you breathe out.*

*Remember these couplets are simply tools to
guide your contemplation or what many call
meditation. Meditation is nothing more than
getting control of your mind. It's prayer. It's
visualization. It's manifesting what you want
to experience in your life. You can "meditate"
while riding your bike or walking to class. You
can "meditate" in a cubical at the library. You
can "meditate" while some unprepared student is
being hammered on a case you know inside out.
Just sit quietly and observe the chatter in your
brain. Then breathe.*

2. SHOW UP

How many times have you heard someone say "I got an interview with somebody I met at the job fair" or something similar and thought, "They get all the luck!?"

You know the feeling. You've had that thought, and so have I. I've been envious of others. It's second-nature to see something you want and work toward achieving that goal. It's why you're in law school.

Good things happen all the time, but only to people who **Show Up**. I'm continually amazed at the number of people who never show up and complain about not getting what they want. I'm amazed at the number of people who never show up at cultural events and complain there's not enough to do. I'm amazed at the number of people who never show up for dinner and complain they have a poor relationship with their family. Look around you. You'll be amazed at the number of students who don't show up for class and complain about the grades they receive.

I'm definitely not preaching to have 100% attendance. As someone who missed my share of classes, I think perfect attendance is a hollow goal. But to be successful you have to show up in your life. You have to *be* there. Sometimes that's enough. You don't always have to have a plan. You don't always have to be the best. But for good things to happen in your life you have to show up to receive them. So how do you decide which things you're going to show up to? It's impossible to physically show up for everything you would like to attend. Obviously, setting priorities is the foundation of showing up.

For me, showing up means saying "yes" to almost every opportunity to give presentations or teach. If I can afford to be there, I go. Almost every business success I've ever received came from saying "yes" when asked to show up. Many times, I simply ask myself if I can pay attention if I go to the event or take on the project. If I can pay attention, I go. If I know I won't be able to pay attention at the event anyway, then I don't go. We'll discuss paying attention in the next chapter.

You'll find your own criteria for accepting opportunities to show up, but remember it's a **conscious** part of finding balance. You have accepted admission to law school. You have identified goals you want to achieve and things you need to change in order to get the most out of your law school experience. Now it's time to follow through.

Accept. Then **Show up**.

3. PAY 100% ATTENTION

Lots of books esplore the topic of paying attention, but few use the title. "Active listening" requires 100% attention. Paying 100% attention to a task is amazingly powerful. Your spouse will light up when he or she knows you are giving them your full attention. Your kids will know the love you feel for them when your mind isn't somewhere else. Your legal clients will know you care when you devote your undivided focus to their issues.

100% Attention is truly "showing up" in each moment of your life and "accepting" the moment as it exists, or accepting your responsibility to change it—or both. To be 100% attentive is to be completely in the moment. It's timeless. When you are 100% attentive there is no past, no future, only the now —which is the only thing we truly ever possess, but almost never appreciate.

Practice

Paying attention is not easy. Your ability to pay 100% attention means truly recognizing and practicing meditation in the context of becoming better at something—like "practicing" the piano.

It takes conscious effort. It takes an understanding that power manifests in silence. The most powerful person in the room is usually the one who says the least, but is the most attentive to the discussion. As one of my mentors (a financially successful and family-conscious man) stated off the cuff one day, "I've found that the more important the decision, the quieter I need to be."

See if you can pay 100% attention to something for even 15 minutes without getting distracted. It's hard. When you can do this you'll find yourself in "the zone" and time will not exist. You will be in the bliss of the moment, and the people who are lucky enough to be with you will feel the power of your full presence.

In law practice, paying 100% attention is what people pay us for. They show up in our office, and they expect us to show up when we're working on their matters. They expect us to be in the room mentally when they're in the room with us physically. Sometimes that's really hard, but when you're conscious that your goal for the next half-hour or hour is to pay 100% attention to that client, then paying attention gets easier. Being patient with them becomes natural.

Why do we get impatient? Because, we aren't mentally in the room. We've already left. We're not paying attention. We're on to our next class, we're on to lunch, we're on to whatever our kids' events will be that evening. Those other things are going to happen anyway so let them go. It doesn't cost anything to bring your attention back to the room. But, you've got to watch for it. Meditative practice helps because it develops control over your thoughts.

Passion

I'm a "big-picture" guy with a clear vision of where I want to be in 10 years and a clear vision of where I want to be in two years. I know what I need to do in the next six months to get to those places. My trouble is staying focused on the tasks of today. They just seem so mundane compared to my big goals, and they're easy to put off until tomorrow. For me, working toward the big picture is far easier than staying focused on the contract I'm reviewing, the corporate bylaws I'm drafting, or the probate work on my to-do list.

I'm in private practice. I can tell people "no." It doesn't hurt me. So I only work with clients who are trying to create something or protect something they've created. If somebody comes along and tries to stomp on my clients' creativity, they're going to get the lion out of me. As lawyers, we have the power and the responsibility to enforce barriers—barriers that protect people, property, and principles. We can support those barriers from a place of power instead of force. That power comes from our passion.

So far, you've identified your goals and priorities for law school. Now comes the mundane burden of actually doing it. You have thousands of pages of case material to read, briefs to write, and myriad other tasks to complete. Some recommend spending at least 50 hours a week on coursework alone. How are you going to pay attention for that length of time every week?

As you go through the mundane, day-to-day work of law school, watch for the things that ignite your passion or arouse your curiosity. Notice when it's easy to pay attention. You will find what you're willing to righteously defend. If you don't find your passion, it will be very hard for you to be happy as a lawyer. For everything else, break it down into smaller chunks.

Parse

I get bored easily. Really bored. Really easily. It's hard for me to pay 100% attention for longer than 30 minutes at a time. So I build my day around clusters of "themes" where I can accomplish big tasks in smaller chunks of 100% attention. I've built my time-management system so that the most I ever expect out of myself is a half-hour of paying attention. How does that work when I block out 90 minutes for an initial consultation? Simple. At a half-hour I'm saying we need to take a little break, get a glass of water, or ask if I can refill their coffee. On the half hour I take a little break, get a glass of water, or ask my client if I can refill their coffee. You might be able to focus longer, and that's great. The message is to know your limits.

On a practical level, you need to be able to get in the zone for up to three hours at a time during essay exams. One of the reasons exams are so anxiety filled is because those three-hour sessions will push your ability to pay attention to one task for an extended period of time. Think about it. If you can't focus for 15 minutes at a time during class, how do you think you'll be at your best for 180 minutes during an exam? Most of the testing tips and tricks for both regular exams and the Bar exam are really ways to break down the exam into smaller chunks such as reading, outlining, prioritizing, writing, and resting before moving to the next question. These are good techniques for life after law school too.

I've taken two Bar exams and passed both. For the first one, it was all I could do to finish the multistate portion in the allotted time. A few months later I sat for the second exam in another state. This time I had studied enough and felt comfortable enough with my ability to finish and pass the exam that I was easily able to take a five minute break every half hour to go to the restroom, splash some water on my face, and refocus my mind on the next half hour. My score shot up. You'll be surprised at how much a very short break can increase your effectiveness in situations that require extreme concentration for extended periods.

Studying law requires 100% attention. Casebooks don't highlight the holding and rule in each case–that's your job. If you aren't paying attention, you will miss the small but crucial phrases that embody the law you are trying to learn.

A friend, who just happens to be a professional coach for lawyers, helped me put this in context. He reminded me that the energy and love we put into each small task is reflected back and expanded like ripples in a pond. As lawyers, we never know when that one clause in the contract, bylaws, or will is going to make a huge impact on the world. In the small day-to-day details, in every moment, we find the potential for big change–if we pay attention.

Accept. Then **Show Up** and **Pay 100% Attention.**

4. MANY IRONS IN THE FIRE

The idea of having many irons in the fire may seem in conflict with the rule of paying 100% attention. It's not. In fact, it's easier to pay 100% attention when you have lots of things to pay attention *to*.

Only a very few of the most highly trained and focused minds can pay 100% attention to one thing for very long. Images of meditating Eastern spiritual masters or Medieval monks at prayer for hours a day come to mind. Sometimes spending hours at a time in meditation, prayer, writing, painting, running, chopping wood, carrying water, hiking, or any other task we enjoy sounds like a wonderful luxury and sometimes like the most boring activity on the planet. We get interrupted. We lose focus. Our minds aren't trained to pay 100% attention to one thing, person, task, or activity for more than a few moments at a time. So, in order to be successful, we need to keep several irons in the fire.

A blacksmith keeps several irons in the fire so that he can pull one out at the right time, focus 100% of his attention on that iron for the time needed, then move to the next iron. When I took a watercolor class in college, we were taught to have several paintings working at once so we could move from one painting to another allowing each to dry appropriately in turn. Almost everything worthwhile takes some time to "dry." Working metal, wood, art, and even writing, needs time to mature into completion.

In the last section we talked about how paying 100% attention is possible when you break things down into smaller chunks. For law school, this means focusing on reading one case at a time, for about 30 to 60 minutes, and refocusing before the next case. Then work on your writing project for an hour or so. Then do the reading for your next class. You get the idea. Get up and move every 30 minutes and be sure to spend a couple minutes looking at something out the window to allow your eyes to rest and refocus at a distance. These little tricks and this approach will make law school more manageable, but it won't make it more pleasant. In order to find balance and happiness, you need to also have other irons in the fire–*in addition to* law school.

Most of us approach life from a scarcity model rather than an abundance model. We only have 24 hours each day or a limited supply of energy. We divide our attention by making trade-offs, multi-tasking, or feeling guilty because we are not able to balance everything the way we "should." In order to break out of the scarcity model, I rely on a concept called "polarity." The principle of polarity states:

> *Everything is dual; everything has poles; everything has its pair of opposites; like and unlike are the same; opposites are identical in nature but different in degree; extremes meet; all truths are but half-truths; all paradoxes may be reconciled.*
>
> The Kybalion

Understanding this principle can be a little tricky, or at least it was for me, but the effort will pay off. For me, it was a big "ah ha" moment in my life. It completely redefined my conceptualization and visualization of "life balance" and "time management."

Polarity requires balance between *related* concepts. That's the trick because most of us spend our time trying to balance *unrelated* concepts. For example, for years I thought I needed to balance my "family" against my "career" against my "spirit" against my "health," etc. It was multi-variable calculus and I never could find the appropriate dynamic state of balance. Something always seemed "off." Then I read about the principle of polarity and a light bulb switched on in my head. I was placing the wrong things at the ends of the poles of my balance control lever. You've probably got unrelated concepts on the ends of your poles of balance right now.

Don't Do This

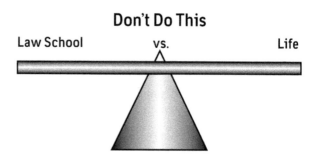

Law School   vs.   Life

Instead of trying to balance unrelated concepts on a teeter-totter, picture a throttle lever on a big airplane. At the bottom is "low" or "no" speed and at the top is "high" speed. One lever controls only one thing–fuel to one engine. This one lever is not trying to control or balance more than one thing.

Likewise, in balancing my life, I needed to visualize the important parts of my life on the appropriate throttles, or "poles." Rather than having "career" at one end of a pole and "family" at the other end of the *same* pole (a zero-sum model where I have to take away from one to give to the other), each area of my life needs a *separate* throttle, with a high and low for "career" on one mental throttle, another labeled "family," another labeled "health", "spirit," etc. This creates an abundance model where I don't have to take away from my family to be doing my best at work. Now, when something feels less than optimal, I know that I've mentally let the throttle slide down and I can mentally visualize pushing that throttle back up *without* letting the other throttle levers slide out of their positions.

Throttles don't necessarily correlate to time or energy or even attention–those are scarce resources. Instead, think of each throttle as measuring your positive intention, your focus *in the moment*, or your drive, desire, and commitment. It's OK to set the throttle on "low," if that's what is optimal for you at that moment in time. In an airplane, the engine only needs full fuel at certain points during the flight. Similarly, law school may only require full throttle during exams. Maybe you have a small child at home or a full-time job or something else in your life that is more important (and deserves to be on "high") than law school. The point is, figure out what the optimal level is for each area so that you can find true balance among all aspects of your life.

You're dealing with a lot of stuff. You're pulled in a hundred different directions at once. Will you focus on Contracts or Property tonight? Will you write that memo or walk your dog? Will you call your mom or your girlfriend? Will you go to the gym or go to the bar for some quality time with friends?

Law school isn't on one end of the pole and life on the other. Instead, law school has its own throttle. You have the power to set it on "high" or "low" or somewhere in between. Picture your control panel and label each throttle or lever. Law school is one lever. Maybe family is another. Friends. Hobbies. Exercise/health. Now focus on each one by itself.

Do This
CONTROL PANEL

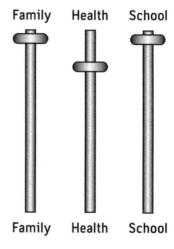

What is the optimal level for that area of your life? Once you've gone through each lever, picture the whole control panel again. It might look something like the wave pattern on your stereo equalizer. That's OK. You don't have to set everything at its highest level. The important thing is to have the proper label placed on each lever and to remember that YOU have the power to set your own controls.

It's no longer a trade-off between family and career. There is plenty of mental fuel for every moment of your life. You don't have to rob energy from one pole to give to another. You just have to pay attention to each iron as you work on it, then simply return it to the fire.

Now, when something feels "off," first ask yourself if you have unconsciously accepted a premise that says you "should" set that throttle at a particular level. If yes, simply *surrender* the negative feelings of guilt and allow yourself to *receive* the positive conviction you have about your choices. If things feel "off" because you have let your own commitment fall below what YOU think is optimal, then simply focus on increasing the mental energy you supply to that throttle. Remind yourself that this is only one of the irons you have in the fire, but for *this moment*, while you are working on it, you must give it 100% of your attention.

Accept. **Show Up**. **Pay 100% Attention** to each of the **Multiple Irons** you have in the fire during the time those irons need your attention, then move on to the next iron.

5. STEWARDSHIP

Every cultural or spiritual tradition gives humans the responsibility for taking care of the planet and each other during their lifetimes. We are accountable for this responsibility through the three keys of stewardship: time, talent, and treasure. Giving back keeps the cycle of surrendering and receiving positively fueled in your life. In order to get, you have to give—you have to make room. Some traditions call this "tithing," but I prefer the term "stewardship" because we are stewards of our existence and caretakers of our world. We live in an interdependent world where everything is connected. When you give, you build the capacity of your community and improve the health of your environment. Then when you are in need, the resources are there to support you in return.

Lawyers have institutionalized this responsibility through pro bono services and systemic encouragement to serve our communities on the boards of nonprofit groups and other civic organizations. We're doing a good job at this, but there is always room for improvement.

Time

Today's fast-paced world makes time the scarcest commodity for many people. Lawyers are no different, law students may have even less time to serve, but when we give our time to a cause that makes a positive contribution, we are "stewards" of our world. Become an orientation counselor for new 1Ls, serve on a student advisory board, sign up for a pro bono project, or volunteer for legal aid. You don't need special skills, you just need to show up. Time is truly a gift from the spirit of your life. Share it.

Talent

Each of us has at least one talent. Lawyers tend to have many. I'm always surprised at how some of the most analytical lawyers in the profession turn out to be some of the most talented musicians or sculptors around. Several law schools hold a "Jam for Justice" fundraising concert every year where students and professors can let their hidden musical talents shine. But you don't need musical talent to give. Maybe you have a talent for financial management, so serve as treasurer; or a talent for gardening, so serve as grounds-keeper. If you're "handy," work on a Habitat for Humanity home. If you're a great writer, be a tutor for underprivileged kids, or a TA for a 1L writing class. If you're a naturalist, lead a scout troop. There are hundreds of opportunities all around you. Think about what you enjoy doing or what you are good at. Then share.

Treasure

Treasure is your money and your possessions. For many, especially lawyers and even more especially wealthy lawyers, writing a check is easier than giving time and talent. That doesn't make giving money less important, because every organization or cause needs financial support to progress toward the fulfillment of its mission. But you might not be in a position to give money right now if you're taking out student loans to cover tuition. So instead, maybe you have a closet full of clothes or a garage full of sports equipment or a basement filled with books or household items you no longer need. Donate those to a local charity. Literally make room in your life for good things to come back to you. *Surrender* your attachment to old possessions and you'll be amazed at the energy you *receive* from having a cleaner house!

Accept what you cannot change and accept responsibility to change your outlook and your life when you can. Consciously choose to **show up** both for your own benefit and for the benefit of others.Pay **100% attention** to what you're doing while you're there, then move on to the next **iron in the fire**. Give back as a way of expressing your **stewardship** of the natural and societal environments in which you live. Keep the conduit for receiving open by surrendering what you no longer need.

Part 2: Putting it All Together

Now that you understand the 5 Guiding Values, let's spend a little time building a framework to actually apply what we've been discussing to your life. Today. Right now.

This section will help you write a manifesto for your life, or at least the next 5 years of your life. We're going to begin at the foundation and move through all five guiding values in an interactive manner. I'll give you some space in the book to write – so write. If you don't want to write here, have a journal ready or open your laptop. I prefer to work in a journal and use a fountain pen to allow just the right balance of reflection and easy speed. Use whatever works best for you, but don't blow this off. Writing down your manifesto may be the single most critical bit of work you will do in your law school career. This exercise can change your life. It will bring you closer to having a successful, and more importantly, happy experience in law school and beyond.

Are you ready to start? Good.

FUEL THE SPARK   *5 Guiding Values for Success in Law School and Beyond*

ACCEPT

Here's the first question: **"What do you accept personal responsibility to change?"**

There are some things you just have to accept as they are. These include your required courses and the way your professors will issue grades. Even so, you still have the power to change your attitude about these "givens," and your attitude directly effects how you experience life. But beyond a few hard and fast specifics, you have the ability to change nearly everything in your life. Of course, practically speaking, you won't be able to tackle everything at once, so you have to make some choices. Where do you start?

First, identify what you are really good at. Where are your core skills?

List them. Be generous with yourself. Fill the next page.

_____

_____

_____

_____

_____

_____

_____

_____

_____

_____

_____

_____

_____

_____

_____

_____

_____

_____

_____

_____

Now, which of those things do you truly love to do?

_____

_____

_____

_____

_____

_____

_____

_____

_____

_____

Of the things you love, **which would you do for free?**

_____

_____

_____

_____

_____

_____

_____

Of the things you would do for free, **which would you actually pay to do**?

_____

_____

_____

_____

_____

_____

_____

_____

_____

_____

Looking at the list of things you would pay your own hard earned cash to do, ask yourself: why not do those things?

You probably think this list has nothing to do with being a lawyer. Here's the connection. Nothing happens by accident. Nothing. You ended up in law school or considering law school for a reason. Whatever that reason is or was, being a lawyer comes down to one thing: helping people.

So here's the big question: How can you combine the things you truly love to do (and would pay to do) with the basic requirement of helping people?

Here's my example.

I love teaching about creative business – always have. Combine that passion for creative business with my legal degree and you have a snapshot of my practice. But take it a step further. At its essence, what I'm doing is helping people reach their creative potential. That's powerful stuff. I believe one of the things we're all here on the planet to do is help each other reach our individual and collective potential. I wrote this book to help you reach your potential so you will, in turn, help somebody else.

Getting a law degree may seem like the fulfillment of your potential but the truth is your full potential is a constantly expanding goal. You will always have new opportunities to grow and help others. To see where to begin, look again at the list of skills you already have and love to use. This is your past. Now think about your future. Who will you help to reach their potential? Define those people right now.

_____

_____

_____

_____

_____

_____

What skills will you need to bring to the table to help those people?

_____

_____

_____

_____

_____

_____

_____

What will you know or do that they won't know or do without hiring you to help?

_____

_____

_____

_____

_____

_____

_____

You now have two lists of skills – those you have and those you need. You have essentially defined the type of work you will accept in your career. This gives you a beacon as you move forward.

SHOW UP

The next step is to figure out how to get from your past to your future by maximizing the opportunities in your present. Look again at the two lists of skills. What classes or other programs (clinics, law review, competition teams) does your school offer that will help you get the skills and knowledge you need to develop and don't have now?

_____

_____

_____

_____

_____

_____

_____

_____

_____

_____

_____

_____

_____

_____

_____

Voila. You just connected your passion to your class schedule. Take a second to absorb what you've done. You now have a road map to help you get the most out of law school so that you will get the most fulfillment out of your career. Your law school may offer too many relevant classes for you to be able to take all of them in three years. Sometimes that really sucks, but if you focus on your goals, by the time the second semester of your third year rolls around you probably won't really care about the classes you missed.

One word of caution - By prioritizing interesting courses you may be tempted to skip some of the "bar exam" classes. Only do that with a great deal of care because having a license is probably going to be a major pre-requisite to reaching your goal of helping people reach their potential. It's not a rule etched in stone – I know several people leading great lives with a J.D. that never sat for the bar. I also know a bunch of people that didn't take a specific "bar exam" course and passed the bar exam with no trouble. For example, I didn't take family law but did fine on both bar exams. My point is, think carefully about which bar classes you want and/or need to take.

Now use the form on pages 58 and 59 to start filling out your 3-year course plan. List the required courses first. Then fill in the electives you would like to take and make sure to plan accordingly for pre-requisite classes. Finally, pray classes will be offered in the semester you need and not at 8am on Monday or 4pm on Friday. Chances are a new seminar will be offered each year that piques your interest. Watch for these opportunities. Hopefully you'll be able to take some classes just for the curiosity factor or because the professor is exceptional. Don't waste any of your time in law school. Use it.

First Year

First Semester	Second Semester
————————	————————
————————	————————
————————	————————
————————	————————
————————	————————
————————	————————

Summer:

————————	————————

Second Year

First Semester	Second Semester
————————	————————
————————	————————
————————	————————
————————	————————
————————	————————
————————	————————

Summer:

————————	————————

3-YEAR PLAN

Third Year

First Semester   Second Semester

_____ _____

_____ _____

_____ _____

_____ _____

_____ _____

_____ _____

Highlight the required courses – Red

Highlight the Bar Exam courses – Yellow

Writing Requirements:

_____ _____

_____ _____

FUN ELECTIVES:

_____ _____

_____ _____

_____ _____

_____ _____

_____ _____

OK, now you're in way better control of your future than you were a few minutes ago. You've made a direct connection between your studies and your skills. You know what kind of work you will accept and you know where you need to show up during law school. Now it's time to examine your ability to follow through.

PAY ATTENTION

Fortunately, when your classes align with your goals, it will be easier to pay 100% attention, but there's still more you can do. Paying 100% attention starts with getting control of your mind. You do that in small chunks. Can you control your mind for a full minute? I bet you can't. Set a timer for 60 seconds and try to hold the picture of your Mom's face in your mind without losing that image for the full time. Try it. It's harder than you think. Your mind is going to jump off and try to give you pictures of your Dad or your siblings or something else. Our minds are very unruly.

Your goal in the next 90 days is to get your mind under control for periods of up to 30 minutes. Why 30 minutes? Because people practice for years and have a hard time focusing for longer than 30 minutes and because if you can focus for 30 minute stretches, there will be no final or bar exam that will ever intimidate you again.

Back to getting control – I cheated a bit telling you to think of your Mom. Moms are emotional triggers that bring up all kinds of mixed feelings. Let's start with something easier. Let's start building a mental picture of your successful self 5 years from now.

In 5 years you will probably have a JD and hopefully be licensed to practice law and help people. If you can't picture that, then we have more work to do than I can cover in this book, so we'll assume you can accept that picture. You've done it, you've successfully graduated from law school, passed the bar, and are pursuing your professional goals.

What does that look like? Picture it. Write a short description, or at least a few key-words or concepts.

Now, what does that feel like? What emotions are you feeling? Pride might be one of them. Confidence might be another. Write about how you will feel when you reflect back on a successful 3 years in law school.

_____

_____

_____

_____

_____

_____

_____

_____

_____

Now, set the timer for one minute again and see if you can hold that picture of your successful self and soak in those wonderful emotions for the full minute.

It was a lot easier wasn't it?

Now let's start adding details. What are you wearing? Where are you working? What kind of car do you drive (if you want to have a car)? What kinds of meetings are you invited to? Who are you working with? Write out the details. Writing these details helps you remember them. It also allows you to control your mind more effectively because you'll be rehearsing the mental picture and soaking in the emotions of success as you add each detail. I was a fine art major as an undergrad, so I like to sketch the pictures. Try being "visual." Try drawing your future success. Go ahead, don't be shy. Nobody will see this but you.

"Houchin, this is all woo-woo metaphysical meditation crap!" you say. Well, maybe it is, but it's worth doing. Visualizations of your future success are useful in at least two ways. First, they keep your success goals top of mind, literally, and help you consciously—and arguably more importantly, unconsciously—move toward that vision. Second, the practice of focusing and adding details to the picture will help you build analytical skills such as the ability to hold both big theoretical concepts and small factual information simultaneously.

Your brain is a powerful tool. When you build mental pictures, you're building an outline from big topics down to small details. Legal analysis works the same way from the big picture of the situation, to the cause of action, to the prima face case, to the facts that build the case, to the case law that cites the precedent. This mental exercise is the core of learning to think like a lawyer and will come in handy no matter what you do. It's also the core of problem solving, which is what lawyers do.

Now set the timer for 5 minutes and try staying in the visualization of your successful self for the whole time. When you can do that without falling asleep, move it up to 10 minutes, then 15. Keep increasing the number of minutes until you can regularly stay in the visualization for 30 minutes at a time. You might find using earplugs or headphones with soft instrumental music very helpful. You'll find that your investment of time in this effort will start helping in your classes and blocks of study time too. Before you know it, paying 100% attention will become second nature.

MANY IRONS

When you can focus 100% of your attention on something for 30 minutes at a time, you'll be far better at managing the multiple irons you have in your life. You'll be focused and productive on the item in front of you without losing productivity because your brain is jumping all over the place. You'll be able to plan and execute your exams. You'll be able to prepare and sit for the bar exam. You'll be able to serve your clients and help them reach their potential. You'll be making huge leaps toward fulfilling and expanding your own potential at the same time.

Even if you balked at drawing pictures, now is the time to get visual. What are the 5 most important areas of your life? Write them here.

Now, let's play with the Law of Polarity. Picture five poles or throttles and label each pole according to your list. Then place a mark on each pole corresponding to where you are today. Are you energized and focused in that area? Are you content and fulfilled? Or are you struggling, unhappy, or simply uncommitted?

MY CONTROL PANEL

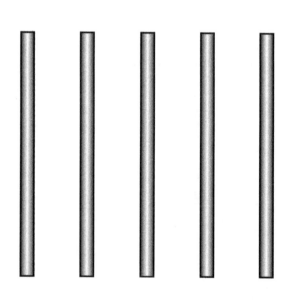

What we're going to do now is hugely important. Mentally visualize yourself pushing each of those marks to the top of the pole. Feel the power flow through you as you move the marks to the top, like pushing a throttle to the hilt or hitting the gas in your car. That power is yours. Pause for a second and notice what it feels like to be at the top of your game in each area. Remember the feeling.

Whenever you feel down about any of these areas in your life, stop and visualize this control panel and mentally push the lever to the max. Feel that power and confidence surge through you even if it only lasts a second.

If it helps, imagine a bar going across the set of levers that locks each at the top setting. Know that you have the power, skill, and confidence to be your best in each area all the time. Abundance is yours, so long as you apply the principle of many irons – focus 100% attention on the one thing that is in front of you now, then move to the next thing.

STEWARDSHIP

When you master the exercises above, you'll have full control over the first four Guiding Values. You'll then be able to find the bandwidth to really start practicing stewardship and giving back to your community.

Look around at the new businesses in your community, especially those formed by young professionals. Most new businesses are aligning themselves with some designated social benefit or organization that receives a portion of their revenue. Get into that habit now. It's not only socially responsible, the right thing to do, and spiritually fulfilling – these days it's good business.

What talents can you share? What possessions can you donate? Where will you give back?

_____

_____

_____

_____

_____

_____

MANIFESTO

Now it's time to write your Fuel The Spark Manifesto. Get out your notes and write this up on pages 70 and 71. If you want a bit more guidance, you will find a PDF on my Web site www.kevinhouchin. com or at www.lawschoolmastermind.com that you can download for free and fill in with your manifesto. You can print it out, laminate it, and carry it in your wallet or purse. You'll also find a set of PDFs that you can use as a screen background or screen saver on your computer. There's also a visual file for your cell phone. Be creative. Be bold. Be proud of the work you have done here.

Of course you can also upload and share your manifesto if you wish, and join the Law School Mastermind community. Just visit www. lawschoolmastermind.com, create an account (the first month's access is free), and engage.

Congratulations! You are well on your way to creating a happier, healthier law school experience. You are also in a position to make a lasting, positive impact on the profession you are about to enter and the world you live in.

Here's to your success.

I Accept:

_____
_____
_____
_____
_____

I Show Up:

_____
_____
_____
_____
_____

I Pay 100% Attention:

_____
_____
_____
_____
_____

MANIFESTO

I keep Multiple Irons in the Fire:

_____
_____
_____
_____
_____

I am a Steward:

_____
_____
_____
_____
_____

APPENDIX: THE POWER OF THE MASTERMIND

Back in the early 1900s, before there was any such thing as professional coaching, a guy named Napoleon Hill started publishing some research. His research was unique. He dedicated his life to interviewing and studying the most successful people of his time: Andrew Carnegie, Thomas Edison, and Henry Ford among others. You may have heard of his books Think and Grow Rich, The Magic Ladder to Success, and The Master-Key to Riches. Think and Grow Rich set the standard by which all modern success manuals are measured.

One of the key concepts to come out of these books was the "Master Mind Group." Think of a Master Mind group as a study group on steroids. Hill defined a Master Mind this way.

A Master Mind may be created through the bringing together, or blending, in a spirit of perfect harmony, of two or more minds. Out of this harmonious blending, the chemistry of the mind creates a third mind, which may be appropriated and used by one or all of the individual minds. This Master Mind

will remain available as long as the friendly,
harmonious alliance between the individual
minds exists. It will disintegrate and all
evidence of its existence disappears the moment
the friendly alliance is broken.

-The Magic Ladder to Success, Napoleon Hill, 1930

A law school study group is a type of Master Mind Group ("MMG"). The goal of a study group is to blend minds and offer mutual support. Unfortunately, many traditional study groups fail in their goal for several reasons including:

1. Competition between members.

2. Divergent interests of members.

3. Lack of leadership.

4. Non-investment by the members.

5. Ignorance relative to how a group works.

6. Lack of content.

7. Difficulty in scheduling.

I didn't like participating in study groups while in law school because I found them to be a waste of time. I had a newborn son and new wife that I wanted to spend time with, so extra time on campus turned me off. I didn't want to take a leadership position in a group because I didn't want to invest a bunch of time helping other members of my class out-do me, and I didn't want to have to pull more than my share of the weight. I was older than most students and didn't want to spend time talking about the dating scene or the parties. And, finally, I had very specific career goals and didn't want to spend extra time hashing through cases that didn't really matter to me beyond a citation in one exam at the end of the semester. All this made me find the traditional law school study group a poor investment of my time.

Contrast this with my friend Kari's experience. She found a group of people who were around the same age and same place in life (married, no kids) and who shared the same level of commitment to their studies. They met after class once a week for about an hour. They each brought questions and took care in helping everyone understand the concepts raised in class. They didn't feel competitive. They each made their own outlines, but did practice exams together. They knew teaching others made them better students. The group was formed during their first semester of law school and although various other people came and went, the four core members stayed committed. In their second and third years they shared fewer classes, but continued to meet on occasion to answer questions and prepare for finals. Each member graduated with honors and they went on to become life-long friends. Their study group was a Master Mind group, even though none of them had ever heard of the concept.

Outside of law school, I've been part of professional Master Mind Groups that really worked and some that didn't reach their goals. The failed groups often started off great, but quickly lost momentum due to some of the same factors listed above.

My goal is for you to experience the benefits that come from participation in a well-run Master Mind Group, because there is overwhelming evidence that when Master Mind Groups work they're incredibly powerful.

www.lawschoolmastermind.com

I've created a new, membership-based, social media Web site called lawschoolmastermind. com. The goal of the site is to help you reach your potential and become successful in law school and beyond.

The site works a lot like Facebook.com, with a chance to engage in social networking with other law students from around the country. You can also access content such as shared course outlines, class notes, join conference calls and listen to audio files that will help you make the most of your law school experience.

The biggest benefit I hope to share with you is the opportunity to participate in or lead a law student Master Mind Group through a system that eliminates the primary causes of failure of law school study groups. An online Master Mind group works better by:

1. Eliminating competition because students are from different law schools all around the country.

2. Creating groups based on shared interests such as substantive areas of law, age, gender, or the geographic location in which you hope to practice.

3. Educating and motivating group leaders to keep the group going. Group leaders will receive access to special group-leader resources such as calls and programming materials.

4. Building ownership through membership fees. When you've paid for something, you show up, so these groups will not fail due to a lack of interest or investment by the group members.

5. Providing audio and ebook resources for both leaders and members about what is expected and how the group works.

6. Offering relevant content to help members create solid groups that will hopefully last a lifetime. Initial programming includes a group-based 5 Guiding Values exercise, Campus Leadership Skills training, and other success-enhancing content.

7. Eliminating scheduling issues by integrating the Web site with text-messaging, email, conference calling, and screen-sharing technologies to make sure you get the full benefit of your membership. Even if you can't make every group interaction, you can catch up "off-line" and still feel active in the group.

Imagine having a set of friends, who will probably become the core of your life-long professional network, who know enough about you to pop you a text or IM right before you head into a Moot Court or Trial Advocacy competition. How great will that feel? Imagine getting some substantive help, such as a review of your law review note or Moot Court brief, from someone you're not competing with for class rank? Finally, imagine the benefit of getting some real practice in helping people.

Take the next step toward your success in law school and beyond. Become a member of lawschoolmastermind.com today.

www.lawschoolmastermind.com

CONCLUSION

The 5 Guiding Values At A Glance:

Accept what you cannot change, then take responsibility for what you can change. Focus on what you want to receive and identify what you must surrender in order to make room for the change you seek. Once you've accepted, you've got to show up. And if you've taken the time to show up, you owe it to yourself and to those around you to pay attention.

Once you're paying attention to *this* then you can move over and pay attention to *that* and keep multiple irons in the fire.

And once you've got those irons in the fire, there are going to be plenty of times where one of the three "Ts" of stewardship is going to be given to you as an opportunity. Take the opportunity to give.

If you keep these values in mind during law school, you'll be far less likely to accept the subtle assumptions prevalent in law school, and you'll definitely be more successful and happy as a law student. You'll have some good things to put down on the "yellow" scraps of paper when thinking back on your law school experience. I'll bet you'll do better on the Bar exam. Most importantly, you'll be far more likely to end up using your legal education in a way that fuels your personal spark of creativity and divinity, and make the world a better place for yourself and all of us sharing this planet with you.

★ ★ ★

Are you being conscious of what you **accept**? Are you being conscious of your outlook, goals, and choices?

Are you **showing up** and **paying attention**? Are you finding your passion?

What **iron** are you working on? Are you getting bored very often?

Are you **being a good Steward**? Where?

Now use the next couple of pages to draft your manifesto.

Go on. Fuel the spark. Succeed!

ABOUT THE AUTHOR

Kevin E. Houchin is an attorney, artist, teacher, author, and principal of Houchin & Associates, P.C. , a copyright, trademark, arts & entertainment, business development, and branding firm located in Fort Collins, Colorado.

To schedule Kevin for keynote speeches, workshops, or seminars, call 970-493-1070 or email kevin.houchin@houchinlaw.com, or visit:

www.kevinhouchin.com.

BUY A SHARE OF THE FUTURE IN YOUR COMMUNITY

These certificates make great holiday, graduation and birthday gifts that can be personalized with the recipient's name. The cost of one S.H.A.R.E. or one square foot is $54.17. The personalized certificate is suitable for framing and will state the number of shares purchased and the amount of each share, as well as the recipient's name. The home that you participate in "building" will last for many years and will continue to grow in value.

THIS CERTIFIES THAT

YOUR NAME HERE

HAS INVESTED IN A HOME FOR A DESERVING FAMILY

1985-2005

TWENTY YEARS OF BUILDING FUTURES IN OUR COMMUNITY ONE HOME AT A TIME

1200 SQUARE FOOT HOUSE @ $65,000 = $54.17 PER SQUARE FOOT
This certificate represents a tax deductible donation. It has no cash value.

Here is a sample SHARE certificate:

YES, I WOULD LIKE TO HELP!

I support the work that Habitat for Humanity does and I want to be part of the excitement! As a donor, I will receive periodic updates on your construction activities but, more importantly, I know my gift will help a family in our community realize the dream of homeownership. ***I would like to SHARE in your efforts against substandard housing in my community!*** *(Please print below)*

PLEASE SEND ME _____ SHARES at $54.17 EACH = $ $_____

In Honor Of: _____

Occasion: (Circle One)   HOLIDAY   BIRTHDAY   ANNIVERSARY

     OTHER: _____

Address of Recipient: _____

Gift From: _____ *Donor Address:* _____

Donor Email: _____

I AM ENCLOSING A CHECK FOR $ $_____ PAYABLE TO HABITAT FOR HUMANITY OR PLEASE CHARGE MY VISA OR MASTERCARD *(CIRCLE ONE)*

Card Number _____ Expiration Date: _____

Name as it appears on Credit Card _____ Charge Amount $ _____

Signature _____

Billing Address _____

Telephone # Day _____ Eve _____

PLEASE NOTE: Your contribution is tax-deductible to the fullest extent allowed by law.
Habitat for Humanity • P.O. Box 1443 • Newport News, VA 23601 • 757-596-5553
www.HelpHabitatforHumanity.org